Table of Contents

Northman Hat

Designed by Sheena Pennell

The Northman Hat is an easy colorwork hat that uses a variegated yarn on a solid background, making it appear much more complicated than it really is! This hat is so fun to knit, you won't be able to make just one.

MATERIALS LIST

SUGGESTED COLORWAY:

Bernat Baby Jacquard's Yarn (90% acrylic, 10% nylon; 346yds/316m per 2.5oz/100g ball) in color #06131 I'm a Big Boy (MC);

1 ball

Deborah Norville Collection Everyday Solid Yarn (100% acrylic; 203yds/186m per 4oz/113g ball) in color #10143170 Black (CC);

1 ball

NEEDLES AND NOTIONS

Size US 4 (3.55mm) 16"/41cm circular needle and set of 4 double pointed needles, or size needed to obtain gauge

Yarn needle

Stitch markers

GAUGE

24 sts and 39 rows = 4" (10cm) in St st

FINISHED MEASUREMENTS

Pattern allows for custom fit.

The pattern repeat for this hat is a multiple of 4 stitches. Measure your head. Multiply this number by 4 to determine cast on amount.

Adjust this cast on number as needed to allow decreases to be spaced evenly as follows: divisible by 8 (small child), 12 (older child), 16 (small adult) or 20 (large adult).

For my hat, I cast on 96 stitches and worked with the 16 stitch decrease. I'll explain more about this later, but it means that when I do the decreases, there will be 6 decrease "spokes" leading to the center of the hat, since 16x6=96.

Knitting the Hat

With MC, cast on desired number of stitches. Pm and join, being careful not to twist the stitches.

Work in k1, p1 rib for 1"/2.5cm.
Knit 1 round.
Switch to CC and begin Chart 1.
Knit 8 rounds in MC.
Work Chart 2.**
Knit 7 rounds in MC.
Work Chart 2.
Knit 6 rounds in CC.
Work Chart 2.
Switch back to MC, knit 1 round.

**Note: Alternatively, you can skip Chart 2 altogether, as well as the strip at the top and knit the body of the hat in a solid color. Simply knit in the round for 4.5"/11cm, then begin the decreases.

Crown Shaping

Note: Change to double pointed needles.

For the decrease rounds, begin as follows:

8 stitch decrease: K6, k2tog.
12 stitch decrease: K10, k2tog.
16 stitch decrease: K14, k2tog.
20 stitch decrease: K18, k2tog.

Pm between each decrease section. Work decrease round every other round, working 1 less stitch before the k2tog each time, until there are 8 stitches left between markers.

For example, with a 16 stitch decrease, the next decrease round would be k13, k2tog, then k12, k2tog, and so on.

When there are 8 stitches left between each decrease, decrease on every row until there are only 2 stitches left between markers. K2tog all the way around until 1 st remains between markers.

Finishing:

Cut the yarn, leaving a 6"/15cm tail. Weave through remaining stitches, pull tight and secure. Weave in ends.

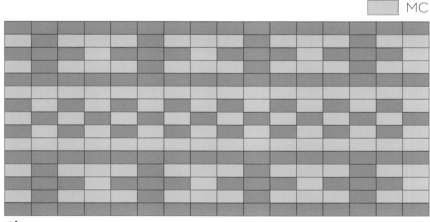

CC
MC

Chart 1

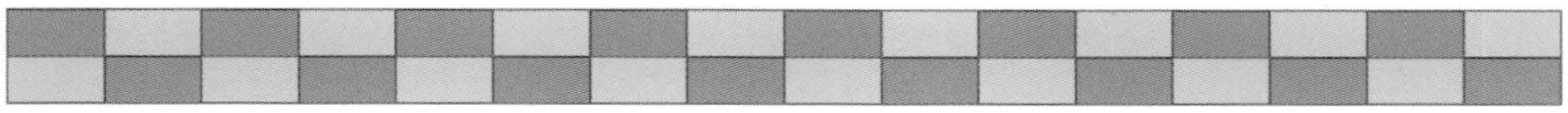

Chart 2

Feather Openwork Beanie

Designed by Kathy North

Hats knit in the round are my favorite projects of all time: they're easy, portable and involve minimal finishing. This lightweight, stretchy cap in mercerized cotton is one result of "playing" with different stitch patterns to create variations on basic hat styles. I used the easy-level feather openwork stitch pattern in two ways: a panel stripe version featuring lacy stripes alternating with plain rounds and an allover version featuring more of the openwork pattern. Knitter's choice!

MATERIALS LIST

YARN

Patons Grace (100% mercerized cotton; 136 yds/125 m per 1.75oz/50g ball) in color # 62140 Spa Blue or # 62246 Leaf

1 (1, 2) balls

NEEDLES AND NOTIONS

Size US 6 (4mm) 16"/41cm circular and set of 4 double pointed needles, or size needed to obtain gauge

Row counter (optional)

Yarn needle

GAUGE

24 stitches and 32 rows = 4" in stockinette stitch

FINISHED MEASUREMENTS

15 (17, 19)"/ 38 (43, 48)cm circumference (will stretch 3-4"/8-10cm)

This beanie is worked in the round from the lower rib to crown. A row counter is useful for keeping track of rounds in pattern.

The pattern is written for the panel stripe version. Instructions for an alternative all-over lace version are included.

Pattern Stitches

Feather Openwork Pattern

(multiple of 5 stitches)
Rnd 1: *K2tog, yo, k1, yo, skp, rep from * around.
Rnd 2: K.
Rep Rnds 1 and 2 for pattern.

Twisted Rib

All rnds: *K1 tbl, p1, rep from * around.

Knitting the Hat (Panel Stripe Version)

With circular needle, cast on 80 (92, 106) sts somewhat loosely. Pm and join, being careful not to twist the stitches.

Rnds 1-8 (twisted rib): *K1 tbl, p1, rep from * around.
Rnds 9-11: K.

Size Small Only
Rnd 12: K.
Size Medium Only
Rnd 12 (dec rnd): *K44, k2tog, rep from * around (90 sts).
Size Large Only
Rnd 12 (dec rnd): K to last 2 sts, k2tog (105) sts.

All Sizes
Rnd 13: *K2tog, yo, k1, yo, skp, rep from * around.
Rnd 14: K.
Rnds 15-20: Rep Rnds 13-14.
Rnds 21-24: K.
Rnds 25-32: Rep Rnds 13-14.
Rnds 33-36: K.
Rnds 37-44: Rep Rnds 13-14.
Rnd 45: K.

Crown Shaping
Note: Change to double pointed needles when needed.

Size Small Only
Rnd 46 (dec rnd): *K38, k2tog, rep from * around (78 sts).
Skip to Rnd 55 and continue through Rnd 69.

Size Medium Only
Rnd 46 (dec rnd): *K13, k2tog, rep from * around (84 sts).
Skip to Rnd 53 and continue through Rnd 69.

Size Large Only
Rnd 46 (dec rnd): *K33, k2tog, rep from * around (102 sts).
Rnds 47, 49, 51, 53, 55, 57, 59, 61: K.
Rnd 48 (dec rnd): *K15, k2tog, rep from * around (96 sts).
Rnds 50, 52, 54, 56, 58, 60, 62, 63, 64, 65, 66, 67, 68, 69: *Knit one fewer stitch per rnd (K14, K13, etc), k2tog, repeating from * around (90 sts, 84 sts, etc) until you reach Rnd 69. *K1, k2tog, rep from * around (12 sts).

Finishing
Cut yarn, leaving an 8" tail. Weave through remaining stitches, pull tight and secure. Weave through ends.

Allover Lace Version

With circular needle, cast on 80 (92, 106) sts somewhat loosely. Pm and join, being careful not to twist the stitches.
Rnds 1-8 (twisted rib): *K1 tbl, p1, rep from * around.

Size Small Only
Rnd 9: K.
Size Medium Only
Rnd 9 (dec rnd): *K44, k2tog, rep from * around (90 sts).
Size Large Only
Rnd 9 (dec rnd): K to last 2 sts, k2tog (105) sts.

All Sizes
Rnd 10: *K2tog, yo, k1, yo, skp, rep from * around.
Rnd 11: K.
Rnds 12-45: Rep Rnds 10-11.
Rnds 46 to end: Following panel stripe version directions, work crown decreases for appropriate size. Finish as instructed in panel stripe version.

Coin Beret

Designed by Gwen Tevis

This project will help you create a slightly slouchy beret with an allover coin-shaped motif created by small cables and yarnovers. This soft hat is perfect for those fall and early spring days when there's a chill in the air, and is a perfect addition to any wardrobe.

MATERIALS LIST

YARN

Sample shown in Patons Angora Bamboo (50% viscose from bamboo, 35% wool, 10% angora; 80yds / 73m per 1.75oz / 50g ball) in color #90046 Urban Grey; 3 balls

NEEDLES AND NOTIONS

Size US 6 (4mm) 16"/41cm circular needle and set of 4 double pointed needles, or size needed to obtain gauge

Size US 5 (3.75mm) 16"/41cm circular needle

Cable needle

Stitch marker

Yarn needle

GAUGE

21 sts = 4" (10cm) in coin patt using larger needles, after blocking

FINISHED MEASUREMENTS

19"/48cm circumference (fits up to 22.5"/57cm head)

Knitting the Beret

Using smaller needles, cast on 128 sts. Pm and join in the round, being careful not to twist stitches. Unless otherwise noted, slip this marker when you encounter it.

Work in K1 tbl, p3 rib for 1.5"/4cm.

Rnd 1: *K1, 1/2 RC, k1, 1/2 LC, rep from * around.
Rnd 2: K.
Rnd 3: *Yo, k2tog, k6, rep from * around.
Rnd 4: K. Remove marker; k1; place marker. The start of the rnd moved 1 stitch to the left.
Rnd 5: *Yo, k6, ssk, rep from * around.
Rnd 6: K.

Rnd 7: *K1, 1/2 LC, k1, 1/2 RC, rep from * around.
Rnd 8: K.
Rnd 9: *K4, yo, k2tog, k2, rep from * around.
Rnd 10: K.
Rnd 11: *K3, ssk, yo, k3, rep from * around.
Rnd 12: K.

Repeat Rnds 1-12 twice more. Repeat Rnds 1-5.

Crown Shaping

Work crown shaping following written instructions below or chart (note: change to double pointed needles when needed).

Rnd 1: *K5, ssk, k3, k2tog, k4, rep from * around (112 sts).
Rnd 2: *K1, 1/2 LC, k1, 1/1 RC, k1, 1/1 LC, k1, 1/2 RC, rep from * around.
Rnd 3: K.
Rnd 4: *K4, yo, k2tog, k4, yo, k2tog, k2, rep from * around.
Rnd 5: *K4, k2tog, k3, ssk, k3, rep from * around (96 sts).
Rnd 6: *K2, ssk, yo, k5, yo, k2tog, k1, rep from * around.
Rnd 7: *K2, ssk, k5, k2tog, k1, rep from * around (80 sts).
Rnd 8: *K1, 1/1 RC, 1/1 LC, rep from * around.
Rnd 9: K.

Rnd 10: *Yo, k2tog, k1, ssk, rep from * around (64 sts).
Rnd 11: K.
Rnd 12: *K1; sl2, k1, psso, rep from * around (32 sts).
Rnd 13: K2tog around (16 sts).
Rnd 14: K2tog around (8 sts).

Cut yarn, leaving a 4"/10cm tail. Weave through remaining stitches, pull tight and secure. Weave in ends.

Finishing

Wet block on a 10" plate to open the coin pattern and form the hat into a slouchy beret shape.

Special Abbreviations

1/2 RC: Sl2 onto cable needle. Holding cable needle in back of work, k1 from left needle. K2 from cable needle.

1/2 LC: Sl1 onto cable needle. Holding cable needle in front of work, k2 from left needle. K1 from cable needle.

1/1 RC: Sl1 onto cable needle. Holding cable needle in back of work, k1 from left needle. K1 from cable needle.

1/1 LC: Sl1 onto cable needle. Holding cable needle in front of work, k1 from left needle. K1 from cable needle.

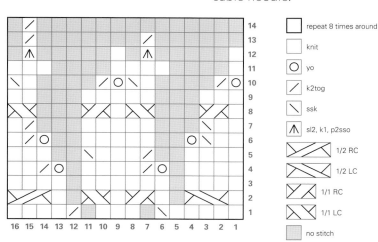

☐	repeat 8 times around
☐	knit
Ο	yo
╱	k2tog
╲	ssk
⋀	sl2, k1, p2sso
	1/2 RC
	1/2 LC
	1/1 RC
	1/1 LC
▨	no stitch

Chill Chasin' Hat

Designed by Ava Lynne Green

Chase away those frigid winter winds with this hat! Knitted with bulky yarn, it has thick, warm flaps that cover your ears to keep out the cold. It's perfect for those icy winter days, whether you're working or playing!

90(100, 110) yds bulky weight yarn

Sample shown in Patons Shetland Chunky (72% acrylic, 25% wool, 3% viscose; 125yds/114m per 3.5oz/100g ball); 1 ball

NEEDLES AND NOTIONS

Size US 10.5 (6.5mm) 16"/41cm circular needle, or size needed to obtain gauge

Stitch marker

GAUGE

14 stitches and 18 rows = 4" (10cm) in slipped rib pattern

FINISHED MEASUREMENTS

18 (20, 22)"/ 46 (51, 56)cm circumference

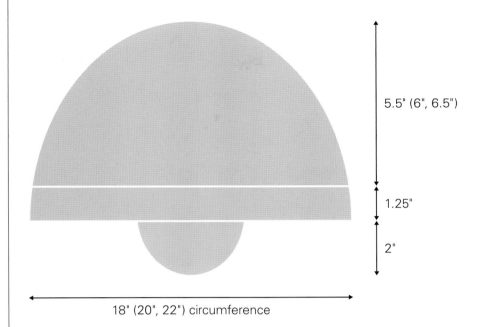

5.5" (6", 6.5")

1.25"

2"

18" (20", 22") circumference

Knitting the Hat

Cast on 64 (72, 80) stitches. Pm and join, being careful not to twist the stitches.

Rnd 1: *K1, p1, rep from * around.

Rnd 2: [K1, p1] 10 (11, 12) times, {wrap, turn the next stitch, [k1, p1] 4 times, wrap, turn the next stitch, * work in rib pattern up to the slipped stitch, work the slipped stitch along with the wrap, wrap, turn the next stitch, work in rib patt up to the slipped stitch, work the slipped stitch along with the wrap, wrap, turn the next stitch *, repeat between the * *s 2 times, work in ribbing patt across the next 14 stitches, work slipped stitch along with the wrap}, [k1, p1] 14 (16, 18) times, repeat between { } one time, [k1, p1] 4 (5, 6) times.

Rnd 3: *K1, p1, rep from * around making sure to work the last two wraps from Rnd 2 together with the stitch.

Rnds 4-6: *K1, p1, rep from * around.

Rnd 7: *K3, slip 1 purl wise, yo, rep from * around.

Rnd 8: K, dropping all yarn overs.

Repeat Rnds 7 and 8 until the hat measures 5.5(6, 6.5)"/14(15, 16)cm from the beg, ending with Row 8.

Crown Shaping

Note: Change to double pointed needles when needed.

Rnd 1: [K3, slip 1, yo, k2, k2tog] 8 (9, 10) times, [56 (63, 70) sts] (after dropping yarn overs).

Rnd 2 and all even numbered rounds: K, dropping yarn overs.

Rnd 3: [K3, slip 1, yo, k1, k2tog] 8 (9, 10) times, [48 (54, 60) sts].

Rnd 5: [K3, slip 1, yo, k2tog] 8 (9, 10) times, [40 (45, 50) sts].

Rnd 7: [K3, k2tog] 8 (9, 10) times [32 (36, 40) sts].

Rnd 9: [K2, k2tog] 8 (9, 10) times [24 (27, 30) sts].

Rnd 11: [K1, k2tog] 8 (9, 10) times [16 (18, 20) sts].

Rnd 13: [K2tog] 8 (9, 10) times [8 (9, 10) sts].

Knit 1 round.

Finishing

Cut yarn, leaving an 8" /20cm tail. Weave through remaining stitches, pull tight and secure.

Weave in ends.

Amelia Earhart Bomber Hat

Designed by Quenna Lee

A daughter's request for a ski accessory with earflaps and pompoms resulted in this slightly oversized bomber hat, reminiscent of the ones worn by the famed aviator, Amelia Earhart. It's quick knit using a single ply bulky yarn, which creates fluffy, cotton ball-like pompoms. By omitting the earflap and pompoms, Amelia becomes a chunky beanie, requiring only one skein.

MATERIALS LIST

YARN

130yds/118m bulky weight single ply yarn

Sample shown in Lion Brand Alpine Wool (100% wool; 93yds/85m per 3oz/85g ball) in color #123 Bayleaf; 2 balls

NEEDLES AND NOTIONS

Size US 11 (8mm) 16"/41cm circular needle and set of 4 double pointed needles, or size needed to obtain gauge

Size US K/10.5 (6.5mm) crochet hook

Stitch marker

Yarn needle

GAUGE

12 sts and 16 rows = 4" (10 cm) in Fishtail Lace patt

FINISHED MEASUREMENTS

24"/61cm circumference

- knit
- ● purl
- ○ yarn over
- ⚠ purl 3tog
- no stitch
- ∗ starting point to PU sts for earflaps

Pattern Stitches

Fishtail Lace (multiple of 12 stitches) or refer to chart:
Rnd 1: *K5, p7, rep from * around.
Rnd 2 and all even-numbered rnds: K.
Rnd 3: *K2, yo, k1, yo, k2, p2, p3tog, p2, rep from * around. **
Rnd 5: *K2, yo, k3, yo, k2, p1, p3tog, p1, rep from * around.
Rnd 7: *K2, yo, k5, yo, k2, p3tog, rep from * around.
Rnd 8: K.
Rep Rnds 1-8 for patt.
** The k1 (between the yarn overs) is for the starting point for picking up the earflap sts.

Garter Stitch
Rnd 1: K.
Rnd 2: P.
Rep Rnds 1 and 2 for patt.

Knitting the Hat

Cast on 72 sts. Pm and join, being careful not to twist the stitches.
Rnd 1: P.
Rnds 2-8: Work in garter st, ending with a k row.
Rnds 9-16: Work one rep of Fishtail Lace patt.
Rnds 17-24: Remove marker, k3, pm, work one rep of Fishtail Lace patt.

Crown Shaping
Note: Change to double pointed needles when needed.
Rnd 25: Remove marker, k3, pm, work Rnd 1 of Fishtail Lace patt.
Rnd 26: K all sts.
Rnd 27: *K2, yo, k1, yo, k2, p2tog, p3tog, p2tog; rep from * around (60 sts).
Rnd 28: K.
Rnd 29: *K2, yo, k3, yo, k2, p3tog, rep from * around.
Rnd 30: K.

Rnd 31: Remove marker, k1, pm. [K7, s2kp] 6 times (48 sts).
Rnd 32: Remove marker, k1, pm. [K5, s2kp] 6 times (36 sts).
Rnd 33: Remove marker, k1, pm. [K3, s2kp] 6 times (24 sts).
Rnd 34: K.
Rnd 35: Remove marker, k1, pm. [K1, s2kp] 6 times (12 sts).
Rnd 36: K.
Cut yarn, leaving a 10" (25.5cm) tail. Weave through remaining stitches, pull tight and secure. Weave in ends.

Earflaps (Worked Flat)
With RS facing up and below the garter rim, pick up and knit 12 sts starting at the k1 [at the yo, k1, yo] and ending at k1 in the following rep.
Rows 1(WS)-7: K.
Row 8: Ssk, k until 2 sts rem, k2tog (2 sts dec).
Rows 9-12: Rep Row 8 until 2 sts rem (2 sts).
Row 13: Remove knitting needle and insert crochet hook. Pull yarn through and single crochet until desired length is reached (sample is 8"/20cm). Cut yarn, leaving an 8"/20cm tail, pull through.
Rep on the opposite side for second earflap.

Pompom (make 3):
Wrap yarn around a 2.5"/6.5 cm width (roughly 3-4 fingers) 30 times. Tie securely in the middle and cut the looped ends on either side. For the third pompom, use a longer length to tie up the pompom.

Finishing
Use 8"/20cm tail of the earflaps to tie pompoms to the end. For the crown, weave the longer ends through the crown and hat. Fluff and trim pompoms to even ends. Weave in ends. Block lightly.

Ruched Cloche

Designed by Hannah Poon

This close-fitting cloche is a soft and simple accessory that's perfect for every occasion. Use yarns in a variety of colors and styles to change up its look - creams and pastels are perfect for spring, while deep purples, maroons and blues make for beautiful fall favorites.

MATERIALS LIST

YARN

Bernat Softee Baby (100% acrylic; 362yds/331m per 5oz/140g ball); 1 ball

Gauge:18 rows of 11 sts = 2"

NEEDLES AND NOTIONS

Size US 2 (3mm) double pointed needles, or size needed to obtain gauge

Yarn needle

1 Large button (optional)

GAUGE

22 sts and 32 rows = 4" (10cm)

FINISHED MEASUREMENTS

19 (20, 21)"/ 48 (51, 53cm) circumference (stretches approx 2"/5cm)

Knitting the Cloche

Cast on 100 (110, 120) sts.

Rnd 1: K.
Rnd 2-3: P.
Row 4: Knit to last st, do not k last st, turn work.
Row 5: Sl first st, Purl to last st, do not purl last st, turn work.
Row 6: Sl first st, Knit to last st worked, do not knit st, turn work (2 sts rem unworked on this side).
Row 7: Sl first st, Purl to last st worked, do not purl st, turn work (2 sts rem unworked on this side).
Row 8: Sl first st, Knit to last st worked, do not knit st, turn work (3 sts rem unworked on this side).
Row 9: Sl first st, Purl to last st worked, do not purl st, turn work (3 sts rem unworked on this side).
Row 10: Sl first st, Knit to last st worked, do not knit st, turn work (4 sts rem unworked on this side).
Row 11: Sl first st, Purl to last st worked, do not purl st, turn work (4 sts rem unworked on this side).
Rnd 12: Turn work, p.
Rnd 13: P.
Rep Row 4 - Rnd13 twice more.
Knit in St st for 3(3, 3.25)"/ 8 (8, 8.5)cm.
P 2 rnds
K 1 rnd.

Crown Shaping

Size Large Only
Rnd 1: *K10, K2tog, rep from * around (110 sts).
Rnd 2: K.
Size Medium, Large Only
Rnd 1: *K9, K2tog, rep from * around (100 sts).
Rnd 2: K.

All Sizes
Rnd 1: *K8, K2tog, rep from * around (90 sts).
Rnd 2, and every other round: K.

Rnd 3: *K7, K2tog, rep from * around (80 sts).
Rnd 5: *K6, K2tog, rep from * around (70 sts).
Rnd 7: *K5, K2tog, rep from * around (60 sts).
Rnd 9: *K4, K2tog, rep from * around (50 sts).
Rnd 11: *K3, K2tog, rep from * around (40 sts).
Rnd 13: *K2, K2tog, rep from * around (30 sts).
Rnd 15: *K1, K2tog, rep from * around (20 sts).
Rnd 17: K2tog around (10 sts).

Cut yarn, leaving an 8"/20cm tail. Weave through remaining sts, pull tight and secure.

Note: Some stitches along ruched short rows may be slightly larger, giving the appearance of holes. These may be fixed by double stitching over these stitches to pull them tighter in line with the gauge for the rest of the hat.

Finishing

With RS facing, pick up and knit 9 sts from bottom ruched edge. Work 6 rows in St st. Bind off loosely, leaving a tail for sewing. Fold strip up over ruched section so purl side is facing out and stitch to hat just above ruching.

Optional: Attach a large button or wooden toggle to this strip as decoration.

Instant Pretzel Hat

Designed by Gwen Tevis

Appropriate for both men and women, this warm winter hat showcases big cables that knit up quickly in chunky yarn. The cables flow from the ribbed brim to the crown, where the decreases are incorporated into the cable motif. This is an excellent project for beginning cable knitters, or for more experienced knitters looking for very quick results.

Lion Brand Wool-Ease Thick & Quick (80% acrylic, 20% wool; 106yds / 97m per 6oz / 170g ball) in color Sky Blue (#106); 1 ball

NEEDLES AND NOTIONS

Size US 11 (8mm) 16"/41cm circular and set of 4 double pointed needles, or size needed to obtain gauge

Stitch marker

Yarn needle

GAUGE

14 sts = 4" (10cm) in K2, p2 rib, unstretched

FINISHED MEASUREMENTS

Adult S/M (L/XL)

18"/46cm circumference [to fit up to 22.5(24)"/57(61)cm head]

Knitting the Hat

Cast on 64 sts. Pm and join, being careful not to twist the stitches.

Work Rnds 1-34 according to the written instructions. Change to double pointed needles when stitches no longer fit comfortably on the circular needles.

Rnd 1: *P1, k2, p1, rep from * around.

Rnds 2-5: Rep Rnd 1.

Rnd 6 (Size L/XL only): [Pfb, *k2, p2; rep from * 3 times, k2, p1] 4 times [64 (68) sts].

Rnd 7: [P1 (2), 2/1 LPC, 2/1 RPC, p2, 2/1 LPC, 2/1 RPC, p1] 4 times.

Rnd 8: [P2 (3), k4, p4, k4, p2] 4 times.

Rnd 9 (Size L/XL only): Rep Rnd 8.

Rnd 10: [P2 (3), 2/2 RC, p4, 2/2 LC, p2] 4 times.

Rnds 11-13: Rep Rnd 8.

Rnd 14: Rep Rnd 10.

Rnd 15: Rep Rnd 8.

Rnd 16 (Size L/XL only): Rep Rnd 8.

Rnd 17: [P1 (2), 2/1 RPC, 2/1 LPC, p2, 2/1 RPC, 2/1 LPC, p1] 4 times.

Rnd 18: [P1 (2), *k2, p2; rep from * 3 times, k2, p1] 4 times.

Rnd 19: [P0 (1), 2/1 RPC, p2, 2/1 LPC, 2/1 RPC, p2, 2/1 LPC] 4 times.

Rnd 20: [P0 (1), k2, p4, k4, p4, k2] 4 times.

Rnd 21: [P0 (1), k2, p4, 2/2 RC, p4, k2] 4 times.

Crown Shaping

Note: Change to double pointed needles when needed.

Rnd 22: [P0 (1), k1, ssk, p3, k4, p3, k2tog, k1] 4 times [56 (60) sts].

Rnd 23: [P0 (1), k2, p3, k4, p3, k2] 4 times.

Rnd 24: [P0 (1), k1, ssk, p2, k4, p2, k2tog, k1] 4 times [48 (52) sts].

Rnd 25: [P0 (1), k2, p2, 2/2 RC, p2, k2] 4 times.

Rnd 26: [P0 (1), k1, ssk, p1, k4, p1, k2tog, k1] 4 times [40 (44) sts].

Rnd 27: [P0 (1), k2, p1, k4, p1, k2] 4 times.

Rnd 28: [P0 (1), k2, p1, k2tog, ssk, p1, k2] 4 times [32 (36) sts].

Rnd 29: *P0 (1), k2, rep from * around.

Rnd 30: [P0 (1), k1, ssk, k2, k2tog, k1] 4 times [24 (28) sts].

Rnd 31: [P0 (1), k1, ssk, k2tog, k1] 4 times [16 (20) sts].

Rnd 32: [P0 (1), ssk, k2tog] 4 times [8 (12) sts].

Rnd 33: *K2 (3)tog, rep from * around (4 sts).

Finishing

Cut yarn, leaving a 4" (10cm) tail. Weave through remaining stitches, pull tight and secure.

Weave in ends.

Special Abbreviations

2/1 RPC: Sl1 onto cable needle. Holding cable needle in back of work, k2 from left needle. P1 from cable needle.

2/1 LPC: Sl2 onto cable needle. Holding cable needle in front of work, p1 from left needle. K2 from cable needle.

2/2 RC: Sl2 onto cable needle. Holding cable needle in back of work, k2 from left needle. K2 from cable needle.

2/2 LC: Sl2 onto cable needle. Holding cable needle in front of work, k2 from left needle. K2 from cable needle.

MATERIALS LIST

YARN

220(240)yd./200(220)m worsted weight yarn

Sample shown in Wool-Ease Worsted Weight (80% acrylic/20% wool; 197 yds/180 m per 3 oz./85g ball) in color #196 Zinnia; 2 skeins

Gauge (in the round): 20 sts and 32 rows = 4" (10 cm) in seed st

NEEDLES AND NOTIONS

Size US 6 (4mm) 16"/41cm circular needle and set of 4 double pointed needles, or size needed to obtain gauge

Size US 5 (3.5mm) 16"/41cm circular needles

Stitch markers

Cable needle

Yarn needle

GAUGE

20 sts and 32 rows = 4" (10cm) in seed st using larger needles

FINISHED MEASUREMENTS

To fit 21-22 (23-24)"/53-56 (58-61) cm head

Sweet Pea Tam

Designed by Quenna Lee

My ambivalence to bobbles was overcome after discovering a miniature version. In this tam, on a seed stitch background, they are embedded in a simple cable stitch, evoking pea pods. Sweet Pea is worked bottom up and available in two sizes.

18

Special Abbreviations

2/2 LC: Sl 2 sts to cable needle and hold in front, k2, then k2 from cable needle.

3-Stitch Bobble
Row 1: K1, yo, k1 (3 sts).
Row 2: P3.
Row 3: K2tog, k1, sl first st over (1 st).

Pattern Stitches

Cable and Mini Bobble (multiple of 6 stitches):
Rnd 1: P1, 2/2 LC, p1.
Rnd 2, 4, 5, 6, 8 and 10-12: P1, k4, p1.
Rnd 3: Rep Rnd 1.
Rnd 7: P1, k1, 3-st bobble, k2, p1.
Rnd 9: P1, k2, 3-st bobble, k1, p1.
Rep Rnds 1-12 for patt.

Seed Stitch (even number of sts):
Rnd 1: *K1, p1, rep from * to end.
Rnd 2: *P1, k1, rep from * to end.
Rep Rnds 1-2 for patt.

K1, p1 Rib (even number of sts)
All rnds: *K1, p1, rep from * to end.

Knitting the Tam

Brim
Using smaller needle, cast on 78 (84) sts. Pm and join, being careful not to twist the stitches. Work in K1, p1 rib until piece measures 1.25" (3cm) from beg. Switch to larger needles.

Body
Increase rnd: Inc 54 (60) sts evenly around [132 (144) sts].
Set-up rnd: K.
Pattern rnd 1: *Work Cable and Mini Bobble patt, work next 16 [18] stitches in seed st; rep from * around.

Rnds 2-48: Repeat Pattern Rnd 1 until four 12-row repeats of the Cable and Mini Bobble patt are completed.

Crown Shaping
In the following rnds, p2tog before and after either the k4 or 2/2 LC in Cable and Mini Bobble patt every odd-numbered rnd unless otherwise noted. Change to double pointed needles when needed. Remove marker, p1, pm for new beg of rnd.
Rnd 49: *Work next 4 sts in established cable patt, p2tog, work in seed st to 2 sts before next 4-st cable section, p2tog, rep from * around [120 (132) sts].
Rnd 50: Continue even in established patt.
Rnds 51-54: Repeat Rnds 49-50 two more times [96 (108) sts].
Rnd 55: *K4, p2tog, seed st for 8 (10) sts, p2tog, rep from * around, [84 (96) sts].
Rnd 56: *K4, p1, seed st for 8(10) sts, p1; rep from * around.
Rnd 57: *2/2/LC, p2tog, seed st for 6(8) sts, p2tog, rep from * around [72 (84) sts].

Rnd 58: *K4, p2tog, seed st for 4(6) sts, p2tog, rep from * around [60(72) sts].
Rnd 59: *2/2/LC, p2tog, seed st for 2(4) sts, p2tog, rep from * around [48 (60) sts].
Rnd 60: *K4, p1, seed st for 2(4) sts, p1, rep from * around.

Size Large Only
Rnd 61: *K4, p2tog, seed st for 2 sts, p2tog, rep from * around (48 sts).
Rnd 62: *K4, p1, seed st for 2 sts, p1, rep from * around.
Rnd 61(63): [K4, p2tog, p2tog] 6 times (36 sts).
Rnd 62(64): [K4, p2tog] 6 times (30 sts).
Rnd 63(65): [Ssk, k2tog, p1] 6 times (18 sts).
Rnd 64(66): [K2, p1] 6 times.

Finishing
Cut yarn, leaving an 8"/20cm tail. Weave through remaining stitches, pull tight and secure. Weave in ends.

Work crown shaping following the chart below

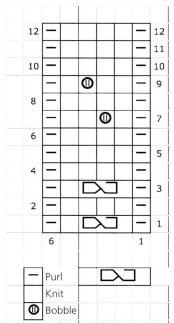

—	Purl
	Knit
⦀	Bobble

2/2 LC (s 2sts onto cn, hold in front, k2, k2 from cn)

**pattern is knit in the round

Whisper Shrug or Cowl

Designed by Suesan Roth

The Whisper Shrug or Cowl is created with kimono ¾ sleeves to make it a great layering piece that is light and airy. The pattern uses a very simple rib stitch used with double knitting, but oversized needles allow the fabric to drape nicely. My sister inspired this piece -- she's often on the go and needs a piece that will flow with her every movement. I wanted her to wear this and, throughout her busy day, feel the whisper of a hug from me!

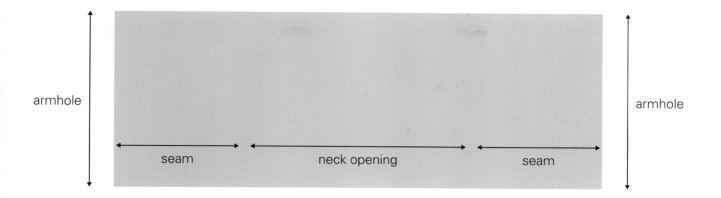

armhole

armhole

seam

neck opening

seam

MATERIALS LIST

YARN

Caron Simply Soft (100% acrylic;
315yds/287m per 6oz/170g ball)
in color #3 Pistachio; 2 balls

NEEDLES AND NOTIONS

Size US 13 (9mm) circular
needle, or size needed to obtain
gauge
Yarn needle
Silk Ribbon (optional)

GAUGE

12 sts = 4" (10cm) in patt

FINISHED MEASUREMENTS

28" wide x 40" long/
71cm x 102cm

Knitting the Shrug/Cowl

Cast on 121 sts using knitted on
cast-on method (it's more flexible).

Row 1: *K1, p1, rep from * to last
stitch, k1.

Rows 2-4: Rep Row 1.

Row 5: Work in seed st for 3 sts,
*K1, p1, rep from * to last 3 sts,
work in seed stitch to end.

Row 6: Work in seed st for 3 sts,
work in K1, p1 rib as set to last 3
sts, work in seed st to end.
Rep Rows 5 and 6 for a total of
108 rows.

Rep Rows 1-4. Bind off in patt.

Finishing

Leave a long tail to sew up sleeve.
Fold in half with right sides facing,
sew edges together along 20
stitches on right side, secure.
Repeat for left side. Weave in
ends.

Blocking

This piece benefits greatly from
a good blocking. Carefully wet
item in the sink, gently squeeze
out excess water, roll in a towel
gently, then set on a dry towel.
Fold in half and pull taut vertically.
We want to keep the double knit
appearance, so you should only
see knit stitches.

Convertible Aran Cowl

Designed by Quenna Lee

The inspiration was to create a cozy cowl that can be worn in multiple ways. A seed stitch border at both ends houses buttonholes and the corresponding buttons. Unbuttoned, it becomes a scarflette, but when buttoned it transforms into a double wrapped cowl. The central lace and cable pattern was chosen to soften the traditional aran design. Note: Cowl uses almost the entire skein; please plan accordingly!

MATERIALS LIST

YARN

150yds worsted weight yarn
Sample shown in Red Heart Mystic (70% acrylic, 30% alpaca; 154yds/141m per 3oz/85g ball) in color #0103 Foam, 1 ball

NEEDLES AND NOTIONS

Size US 7 (4.5mm), or size needed to obtain gauge
Two ¾"(2cm) diameter buttons
Yarn needle

GAUGE

20 sts and 32 rows = 4" (10cm) in seed stitch

FINISHED MEASUREMENTS

4.5" wide x 41" circumference/ 11cm x 104cm

Pattern Stitches

Seed Stitch (multiple of 2 +1 stitches):
All rows: *K1, p1; rep from * to last st, k1.

Cable Eyelet Pattern (multiple of 21 sts) or refer to chart:
Row 1: P1, 3/2 RC, p2, [ssk, yo] 2 times, k1, p2, 3/2 RC, p1.
Row 2: K1, [p5, k2] 2 times, p5, k1.
Row 3: P1, k5, p2, [ssk, yo] 2 times, k1, p2, k5, p1.
Row 4: Rep Row 2.
Row 5: Rep Row 1.
Row 6: Rep Row 2.
Row 7: P1, [k5, p2] 2 times, k5, p1.
Row 8: Rep Row 2.
Row 9: P1, [ssk, yo] 2 times, k1, p2, 3/2 RC, p2, [ssk, yo] 2 times, k1, p1.
Row 10: Rep Row 2.
Row 11: P1, [ssk, yo] 2 times, k1, p2, k5, p2, [ssk, yo] 2 times, k1, p1.
Row 12: Rep Row 2.
Row 13: Rep Row 9.
Rows 14-16: Rep Rows 6-8.
Rep Rows 1-16 for patt.

Knitting the Cowl

Note: Sl first st unless otherwise noted.

Tapered edging:

Cast on 23 sts.
Work in seed st for 7 rows, ending with a WS row.
Next (inc) row (RS): Work in patt, inc 1 st each end of row (25 sts).
Next row: Work even.
Rep last 2 rows once more (27 sts).

Body

Pattern Row 1: Work seed st for 3 sts, work Cable Eyelet patt, work seed st for 3 sts.
Work as set until piece measures 41"/104cm.

Next (dec) row (RS): Begin seed st patt, dec 1 st each end of row (25 sts).
Next row: Work even.
Rep last 2 rows once more (23 sts).
Next row: Work 6 sts of patt as established, yo, dec (K2tog or p2tog as appropriate), maintain patt until 7 sts left, yo, dec, work in patt to end.
Work even in patt for 4 rows more.
Bind off in pattern.

Finishing

Weave in ends. Block. Sew buttons opposite buttonholes.

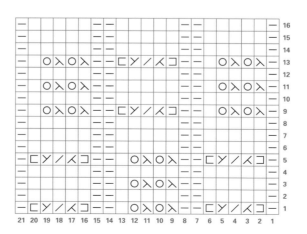

RS knit **WS** purl
— **RS** purl **WS** knit
O yarn over
⋋ ssk
⊏⋋╱⋌⊐ **3/2 RC** sl2 to cn, hold in back, k3, k2 from cn

Twisted Zig-zag Scarf

Designed by Denise Twum

For this scarf, I used a simple knit/purl alternation to create a zigzag pattern with a twist, so that the zigzag lines that snake across the scarf stand in nice relief against the stockinette background. A 2-stitch mock cable works as the border on either side of the scarf, framing the zigzag pattern. The versatility of this pattern means that it can be adapted and used for various articles such as a scarf, a baby blanket, or an afghan.

MATERIALS LIST

YARN

Bernat Roving (80% acrylic, 20% wool; 120 yd/109 m per 3.5oz/100g ball) in color #00032 Putty, 2 skeins

NEEDLES AND NOTIONS

Size US 11 (8mm) straight needles, or size needed to obtain gauge
Markers
Stitch holders
Yarn needle

GAUGE

8 sts and 11 rows = 4" (10cm) in patt

FINISHED MEASUREMENTS

10" wide x 78" long/ 25cm x 198 cm

Special Abbreviations

RFC: Knit into the 3rd stitch on the left needle without slipping stitch off left needle. Knit the first and 2nd stitches as usual, slipping them off as you knit them. Slip off the 3rd stitch.

Pattern Stitches

Zig Zag (multiple of 24 stitches) or refer to chart:

Row 1: K4, p1, [k5, (p1 tbl) 2 times] twice, p1, k3, slip st wyif.
Row 2: K1, p3, k1, p1, [k1 tbl] 2 times, p5, [k1 tbl] 2 times, p4, k1, p3, slip st wyib.
Row 3: K1, RFC, p1, k3, [p1 tbl] 2 times, k5, [p1 tbl] 2 times, k2, p1, RFC, slip st wyif.
Row 4: K1, p3, k1, p3, [k1 tbl] 2 times, p5, [k1 tbl] 2 times, p2, k1, p3, slip st wyib.
Row 5: K4, p1, k1, [p1 tbl] 2 times, k5, [p1 tbl] 2 times, k4, p1, k3, slip st wyif.
Row 6: K1, p3, k1, [p5, (k1 tbl) 2 times] twice, k1, p3, slip st wyib.
Row 7: K1, RFC, p1, [(p1 tbl) 2 times, k5], p1, RFC, slip st wyif.
Row 8: K1, p3, k1, p4, [k1 tbl] 2 times, p5, (k1 tbl)2x, p1, k1, p3, slip st wyib.
Row 9: K4, p1, k2, [p1 tbl] 2 times, k5, [p1 tbl] 2 times, k3, p1, k3, slip st wyif.

Row 10: k1, p3, k1, p2, [k1 tbl] 2 times, p5, [k1 tbl] 2 times, p3, k1, p3, slip st wyib.
Row 11: K1, RFC, p1, k4, [p1 tbl] 2 times, k5, [p1 tbl] 2 times, k1, p1, RFC, slip st wyif.
Row 12: K1, p3, k1, [k1 tbl] 2 times, p5, [k1 tbl] 2 times, p5, k1, p3, slip st wyif.
Rep Rows 1-12 for patt.

Knitting the Scarf

Cast on 24 sts. Work in patt until piece measures 78"/198cm.
Bind off.

Finishing
Weave in ends. Block.

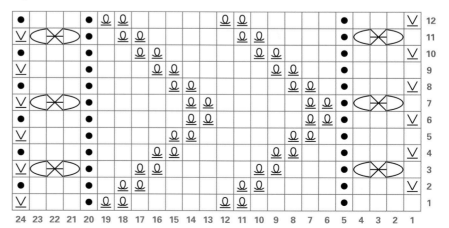

		RS knit WS purl
	●	RS purl WS knit
	Ω	RS p1 tbl WS k1 tbl
	⊗	RS right front cross WS purl
	V	RS slip with yarn in front WS yarn in back

Nordic Inspired Cowl

Designed by Susan Anderson-Freed

One of my dog walking routes takes me through a large barren trail where the winter wind burns my face and neck. It always found ways to enter through the folds in my scarves, and I didn't realize at the time that a cowl was the solution to my problem. This cowl features a double hem, providing an extra layer of warmth for your face. The first (hidden) selvedge uses stockinette stitch, and the second (inside) selvedge uses the repeating pattern.

MATERIALS LIST

YARN

Lion Brand Wool-Ease Worsted Weight (80% acrylic/20% wool; 197yds/180m per 3 oz./85g ball) in colors #153 Black (1 ball), #151 Grey Heather (1 ball), #138 Cranberry (1 ball), #118 Indigo (1 ball), #139 Dark Rose Heather (1 ball), #402 Wheat (1 ball), #501 White Frost (1 ball)

Note: There will be just enough White Frost to finish one cowl.

NEEDLES AND NOTIONS

Two Size US 4 (3.5mm) 24"/61cm circular needles or set of 4 double pointed needles

Gauge
6.5 sts x 6.5 rnds per 1"(2.5cm) square

FINISHED MEASUREMENTS

10.5" x 22" circumference/ 27cm x 56cm circumference

Knitting the Cowl

Cast on 130 sts using White Frost.

Selvedge: Knit 4 rnds in White Frost.
Hem: Purl one rnd. Knit 3 rnds in White Frost, increasing 14 sts on the 2nd rnd (144 sts).
Bottom Inside Pattern: Knit the 13 rnd bottom inside pattern.
Small Motif: Knit the 17 rnd small motif pattern.
Large Motif: Knit the 35 rnd large motif pattern.
Small Motif: Knit the 17 rnd small motif pattern.
Top Inside Pattern: Knit the 13 rnd top inside pattern.
Knit 3 rnds in White Frost, decreasing 14 sts on the second rnd.

Hem: Purl one rnd.
Selvedge: Knit 4 rnds in White Frost.

Finishing

Bind off. Turn the hem to the inside and tack into place. Turn the bottom inside pattern to the inside and tack into place. Repeat for the top inside pattern. Weave in all ends. Block.

- ■ Black
- ■ Indigo
- ■ Cranberry
- ■ Dark Rose Heather
- ▢ Wheat
- ▢ Grey Heather
- ☐ White Frost

Small Motif

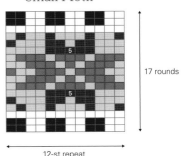

17 rounds

12-st repeat

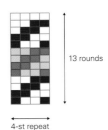

13 rounds

4-st repeat

Bottom Inside Pattern

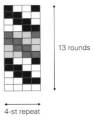

13 rounds

4-st repeat

Top Inside Pattern

Large Motif

35 rounds

36 sts

Nautical Scarf

Designed by Denise Twum

This scarf was borne out of a desire to knit a simple garter stitch scarf that looked fancy but was actually simple to execute. Simple striping at regular intervals provides one design on one side of the scarf, and a different design on the other side. This customizability makes it a great unisex pattern, and will make a wonderful gift for men.

MATERIALS LIST

YARN

Lion Brand Vanna's Choice (100% acrylic; 170 yd/156 m per 3.5oz/100g ball) in colors:
#125 Taupe, 3 balls (MC)
#170 Pea Green, 1 ball (CC)

NEEDLES AND NOTIONS

Size US 15 (10mm) 29"/74cm circular needle, or size needed to obtain gauge
Yarn needle
Size US J/10 (6 mm) crochet hook

GAUGE

7 sts and 12 rows = 4" (10cm) in garter stitch

FINISHED MEASUREMENTS

8" wide x 108" long/ 20cm x 274cm

Knitting the Scarf

Cast on 190 sts loosely with MC held doubled.

Rows 1-4: Knit 4 rows.
Row 5: Switch to single strand of CC. Knit one row.
Row 6: Slide stitches to other end of needle where MC strands are hanging, and knit 1 row with MC.
Rows 7-9: Knit with MC.
Row 10: Slide stitches to other end of needle where CC strand is hanging, and knit 1 row.

Repeat these 10 rows 2 more times (for a total of 3 repeats), then work Rows 1- 4 one more time. Bind off loosely.

Finishing
Fringe (on short ends of scarf):
Cut 60 pieces of CC yarn, each 16"/41cm long. Each fringe will have 6 pieces of CC yarn.

Insert the crochet hook through one corner of the short edge, pull the 6 pieces of CC yarn through and tie off to create a fringe.

Measure off 2"/5cm on the scarf edge, and create another fringe at the 2"/5cm spot. Continue in this way until 5 fringes have been created on that end.

Repeat on the other short edge.

Weave in ends. Block.

Nautical Cowl

Designed by Denise Twum

The cowl is knit sideways from one tip to the other and seamed at the ends to form the circular shape, but it can also be left as a scarf without joining the ends. The final decorative touch is a row of single crochet edging worked in the contrast color to make the cowl pop.

MATERIALS LIST

YARN

Lion Brand Vanna's Choice (100% acrylic; 170 yd/156 m per 3.5oz/100 g ball) in colors:

#171 Fern, 3 balls (MC)
#140 Dusty Rose, 1 balls (CC)

NEEDLES AND NOTIONS

Size US 15 (10mm) 29"/74cm circular needle, or size needed to obtain gauge
Ring stitch marker
Yarn needle
Size US J/10 (6mm) crochet hook

GAUGE

9 rows = 4" (10cm) in patt

FINISHED MEASUREMENTS

9" wide x 64" circumference/ 23cm x 162cm

Knitting the Cowl

Cast on 3 sts loosely with MC held doubled.

Setup:
Rows 1-4, 6-9: Knit in MC.
Rows 5 and 10: Knit in single strand of CC.

Increase Section
Rows 1,3,5,7,9: Kfb, k to last st, kfb (2 sts inc).
Rows 2,4,6,8,10: K.
Repeat Rows 1-10 once more for a total of 20 rows (23 sts).

Main Body Section
Note: Work in colors as follows -
Rows 11-14, 16-19: Knit in MC.
Rows 15 and 20: Knit in CC.

Rows 11, 13, 15: K1, kfb, k to last 3 sts, k2tog, k1.
Rows 12,14,16,18,20: K.
Rows 17 and 19: K1, ssk, k to last 2 sts, kfb, k1.

Repeat these 10 rows eleven more times for a total of 12 repeats.

Decrease Section
Row 21: K1, k2tog, k to last 3 sts, k2tog, k1 (2 sts dec).
Row 22: K.

Repeat these two rows until there are 5 stitches left on the needle.
Next row: K1, k2tog, k2tog (3 sts).
Last row: K3tog. Bind off.

Finishing
Block to measurements. Sew short ends together. With crochet hook, work 1 round of single crochet along top and bottom edges. Weave in ends.

Interlocking Leaves Scarf

Designed by Quenna Lee

Interlocking Leaves is a knitter's take on the popular bulky scarves. It is a rectangular scarf, long enough to wrap doubly around the neck. The alternating panels of interlocking leaves and garter eyelet provide drape and visual interest. Varying stitch counts are used to accommodate the differences in gauge.

MATERIALS LIST

YARN

150yds bulky weight yarn
Sample shown in Lion Brand
Wool-Ease Chunky (80% acrylic,
20% wool; 153yds/140m per
5oz/140g ball) in color
#130 Grass, 1 ball

NEEDLES AND NOTIONS

Size US 11(8mm), or size needed
to obtain gauge
Yarn needle

GAUGE

11 sts = 3.5" (9cm) in patt

FINISHED MEASUREMENTS

5.5" wide x 70" long/
14cm x 178cm

Pattern Stitches

Interlocking Leaves (multiples of
11 sts) or refer to chart:
Row 1: K6, k3tog, yo, k1, yo, k1.
Row 2 and all even rows: P.
Row 3: K4, k3tog, k1, yo, k1, yo, k2.
Row 5: K2, k3tog, k2, yo, k1, yo, k3.
Row 7: [K1, yo] 2 times, sl1,
k2tog, psso, k6.
Row 9: K2, yo, k1, yo, k1, sl1,
k2tog, psso, k4.
Row 11: K3, yo, k1, yo, k2, sl1,
k2tog, psso, k2.
Row 12: P.
Rep Rows 1-12 for patt.

Garter Eyelet (multiple of 17 sts):
Row 1 (dec row): K1, k2tog, k11,
k2tog, k1 (15 sts).
Rows 2-4, 6, 8: K.
Row 5: K1, (yo, k2tog) to end.
Row 7 (inc row): K1, kfb, k11, kfb, k1
(17 sts).
Rep Rows 1-8 for patt.

Knitting the Scarf

Slip first st of each row unless
otherwise noted.
Cast on 13 sts.

Tapered garter edging:
Row 1: K.
Row 2: K1, kfb, k9, kfb, k1 (15 sts).
Row 3: K.
Row 4: K2, kfb, k9, kfb, k2 (17 sts).

Body (keep first and last 3 sts in
garter st):
Row 1: K3, work Interlocking
Leaves patt, k3.
Rows 2-24: Work as set until
two repeats of the Interlocking
Leaves patt are completed.
Row 25: Work Garter Eyelet
patt.
Rows 26-32: Work as set until
one rep of Garter Eyelet patt
is completed.
Rows 33-224: Rep Rows 1-32 six
times.
Rows 225-248: Rep Rows 1-24
once.

Tapered garter edging:
Row 1: K2, k2tog, k9, k2tog, k2
(15 sts).
Row 2: K.
Row 3: K1, k2tog, k9, k2tog, k1
(13 sts).
Row 4: K.
Row 5: Bind off.

Finishing
Weave in ends. Block.

☐	**RS** knit **WS** purl
Ο	yarn over
Λ (k3tog)	k3tog
λ (sl1, k2tog, psso)	sl1, k2tog, psso

General Knitting Information

In the instructions for the projects, I have favored US knitting terms.
Refer to this box for the UK equivalent.

US Term
bind off
gauge
stockinette stitch
reverse stockinette stitch
seed stitch
moss stitch

UK Term
cast off
tension
stocking stitch
reverse stocking stitch
moss stitch
double moss stitch

Yarn Weight Guidelines

Since the names given to different weights of yarn can vary widely depending on the country of origin or the yarn manufacturer's preference, the Craft Yarn Council of America has put together a standard yarn weight system to impose a bit of order on the sometimes unruly yarn labels. Look for a picture of a skein of yarn with a number 0–6 on most kinds of yarn to figure out its "official" weight. The information in the chart below is taken from www.yarnstandards.com.

	SUPER BULKY (6)	BULKY (5)	MEDIUM (4)	LIGHT (3)	FINE (2)	SUPERFINE (1)	LACE (0)
WEIGHT	super-chunky, bulky, roving	chunky, craft, rug	worsted, afghan, aran	light worsted, DK	sport, baby, 4ply	sock, fingering, 2ply, 3ply	fingering, 10-count crochet thread
KNIT GAUGE RANGE*	6–11 sts	12–15 sts	16–20 sts	21–24 sts	23–26 sts	27–32 sts	33–40 sts
RECOMMENDED NEEDLE RANGE**	11 (8mm) and larger	9 to 11 (5.5–8mm)	7 to 9 (4.5–5.5mm)	5 to 7 (3.75–4.5mm)	3 to 5 (3.25–3.75mm)	1 to 3 (2.25–3.25mm)	000 to 1 (2–2.25mm)

Notes: * Gauge (tension) is measured over 4in/10cm in stockinette (stocking) stitch
** US needle sizes are given first, with UK equivalents in brackets

Substituting Yarns

If you substitute yarn, be sure to select a yarn of the same weight as the yarn recommended for the project. Even after checking that the recommended gauge on the yarn you plan to substitute is the same as for the yarn listed in the pattern, make sure to knit a swatch to ensure that the yarn and needles you are using will produce the correct gauge.